Salvation

Is

Key

By: Brenda Taylor

Table of contents

Introduction

This book is for those who are lost, struggling with feelings of hopelessness, depression, and despair. If you're merely going through the motions of life and feel like there's no hope for tomorrow, I'm here to tell you that there is hope in Jesus. Throughout these pages, you will discover more about our blessed Savior, Jesus Christ, and gain a deeper understanding of what salvation truly means.

Chapter 1

Salvation is Key

If you've come across this book, I want you to know that God loves you, and there is hope. More than 2000 years ago, God sent His only begotten Son, Jesus, to die on the cross for your sins and the sins of this whole wide world. If you're feeling lost, as if there is something missing in your life, a void you cannot seem to fill with worldly things, I'm here to tell you that what you're indeed missing is Jesus. He's calling you near to Him today. If you feel like life isn't worth living and there's no hope for tomorrow, there is.

Let me share a chapter of my life with you. It's 1982 I was newly married and was very happy, yet I felt like there was something deeply missing in my life. I would oftentimes sit and wonder about my soul, and if I died unsaved, where would my soul go.

One day I was sitting in my living room watching tv when a minister came on and extended the invitation to salvation to anyone viewing the program. At that time, I felt very empty and void on the inside. I knew something was missing in my life. The preacher on the tv screen asked if there was anyone watching who felt a tugging at their heart to accept Jesus as their personal Lord and Savior. That person was me. I knew it was God calling me to come to Him. I prayed the sinner's prayer with a sincere heart because I was tired of living a life of sin. I was tired of always wondering about my soul and never knowing the answer. Upon accepting Jesus Christ, a transformative wave swept through my life. It marked a turning point, and in that moment, I made a promise to God that I would serve Him and never turn back. Life hasn't always been easy since then, but I've remained steadfast in keeping that promise. If you, too, sense God tugging at your heart, I implore you not to dismiss or resist that gentle pull. I invite you to dive deeper into the pages of this book, where you can discover the essence of Salvation, the role of Jesus, and the profound meaning of Christianity.

So many people believe that salvation is challenging, but it's not. It's one of the easiest things to obtain but the key is that it must be done with a sincere heart. My personal experience in the living room, watching the minister on TV, was an intimate moment between me and Jesus. I opened my heart sincerely and offered a prayer. It wasn't about crafting an elaborate oration; instead, I came to Him as I was, in all my brokenness and He heard me. He will hear you too.

The True Meaning of Salvation

Salvation means to be saved by God from the consequences of sin. You might wonder why you need saving from these consequences. It's quite simple. The bible states in Romans 6:23, *"For the wages of sin is death; but the gift of God is eternal life through Jesus Christ our Lord."* This means that the payment or punishment for sin is death and eternal separation from God. This same scripture also lets us know that God gives us the gift of eternal life through Jesus Christ. Eternal life means to spend all eternity with Jesus in heaven.

Salvation can be achieved in five easy steps:

1. Acknowledgment (willingly admitting that you're a sinner in need of salvation).
2. Repentance (turning away from your sins).
3. Confession (acknowledging that you have lived a sinful life).

4. Forgiveness (asking God to forgive you of all your sins).
5. Forsake (giving up all your sinful desires and following Jesus).

Romans 10:9-10 states, *"That if thou shalt confess with thy mouth the Lord Jesus, and shalt believe in thine heart that God hath raised him from the dead, thou shalt be saved. For with the heart man believeth unto righteousness; and with the mouth confession is made unto salvation."*

Salvation is something that can't be bought, it is actually a free gift offered to you from God Himself. I always tell people, "You can't buy it for $19.99, and it never goes on sale." Jesus paid the ultimate price for our salvation. You don't have to be good or perfect in order to receive salvation. God wants you to come to Him in your present state and He will do the changing. He already knows that humanity has a sinful nature. He desires us to bring all our problems, bad habits, addictions, etc., to Him. Matthew 9:13 says, *"But go ye and learn what that meaneth, I will have mercy, and not sacrifice: for I am not come to call the righteous, but sinners to repentance."*

Who is Jesus Christ?

As we navigate the depths of salvation and experience the transformative mercy of our gracious God, a curiosity emerges: "Who is Jesus Christ?" This compelling question draws us into the very essence of our Christian journey, revealing Jesus as the Son of God, the second person in the Holy Trinity.

The Trinity is a profound concept that unveils the intricate nature of God, presenting Him as three in one. While God is a singular essence, He manifests in three distinct persons, each bearing unique characteristics: God the Father, God the Son, and God the Holy Spirit. Together, they form the Holy Trinity. In the person of Jesus Christ, we witness an extraordinary union of divinity and humanity. Jesus, the God-man, is fully God and fully man, conceived by the Holy Spirit and born of the Virgin Mary, harmonizing divine and human elements perfectly. As Luke 1:35 aptly puts it, *"The Holy Ghost shall come upon thee, and the power of the Highest shall overshadow thee: therefore also that holy thing which shall be born of thee shall be called the Son of God."*

The narrative of Jesus's birth, as recounted in Matthew 1:18, 20, further emphasizes the miraculous nature of His conception, reassuring Joseph, Mary's husband, that what is conceived in Mary is of the Holy Ghost.

"Now the birth of Jesus Christ was on this wise: When as his mother Mary was espoused to Joseph, before they came together, she was found with child of the Holy Ghost. But while he thought on these things behold, the angel of the LORD appeared unto him in a dream, saying, Joseph, thou son of David, fear not to take unto thee Mary thy wife: for that which is conceived in her is of the Holy Ghost." This divine origin underscores the unique blend of divinity and humanity found in Jesus."

Beyond His divine nature, Jesus stands as a representation of God's heart, embodying God's unconditional love for humanity. This profound love is beautifully captured in John 3:16: *"For God so loved the world that He gave His only begotten Son, that whosoever believeth in Him should not perish but have everlasting life."* Through Jesus, we glimpse the depth of God's love, a love that surpasses all understanding and extends an invitation to everlasting life for those who believe in Him.

This love story finds its roots in Genesis 2:16-17, when God instructed Adam not to eat from the tree of the knowledge of Good and Evil, warning that disobedience would lead to death.

Fast forward to Genesis 3:4-7, where Adam and Eve, influenced by the serpent in disguise, chose disobedience, introducing sin into the world. This disobedience not only severed the connection between man and God but also led to the unintentional transfer of earthly authority to satan, who became the prince of the air.

The debt owed to God by Adam and Eve for their disobedience could never be satisfied until Jesus, both fully God and fully man, came to earth. Born of the Virgin Mary, Jesus gave His life on the cross as a ransom for humanity. This sacrificial act was the only means for unholy humanity to be reconciled to holy God. As Jesus was crucified, He became the sacrificial lamb, paying the debt incurred by Adam and Eve's sin in the Garden of Eden. His death on the cross fully satisfied our sin debt.

Now, all who believe in Him and turn to Him can be saved from a world of sin and receive the precious gift of eternal life. Through the redemptive work of Jesus, God's love not only offers salvation but also restores the authority that was lost, providing a path for humanity to once again be in a harmonious relationship with God. This profound love story prompts a crucial reflection on the destination of our souls.

Come to Jesus While You Still Can

Do you know what happens after you die? Some people think that they just sleep forever, everything fades to black like a tv screen and that's the end of things. Many people don't have a clue about what happens to their soul after death.

Consider this question: If you were to pass away tonight, without seeing tomorrow's light, do you know where your soul would spend eternity? Do you understand what a soul is? Your soul is the essence of who you are, it consists of your will, your intellect, your emotions, and your memory and it will never die; it persists beyond death. Luke 16:19-31 tells a parable of Lazarus and the rich man, illustrating the consequences of knowing or not knowing God. The rich man, living without knowledge of God, ended up in hell, while Lazarus, who knew God, ascended to heaven.

You don't want to follow the rich man's path. Your soul, the most precious possession, will determine your eternal destination—either in heaven or hell. The Bible emphasizes the urgency of making preparations while you are alive, as there is no repentance beyond the grave (Hebrews 9:27). Judgment comes after death, and none will have the chance to profess belief once facing it.

For we must all appear before the judgment seat of Christ; that every one may receive the things done in his body, according to that he hath done, whether it be good or bad (2 Corinthians 5:10).

God, omnipresent and all-knowing, sees every hidden aspect of our lives, judging the thoughts of our hearts. It's crucial to repent and turn away from wicked ways, as nothing in this life is worth an eternity in hell.

Don't Procrastinate

Many good people have said to themselves, "I will give my life to Jesus when I get old," but never make it to old age. Their life is cut off prematurely. Please do not assume you have more time than you do. Death can come unexpectedly, and at that point, it's too late. Jesus emphasized the significance of being prepared through a parable about wise and foolish virgins. The wise ones, prepared with oil for their lamps, entered the marriage feast, while the foolish missed the opportunity.

Then shall the kingdom of heaven be likened unto ten virgins, which took their lamps, and went forth to meet the bridegroom. And five of them were wise, and five were foolish. They that were foolish took their lamps, and took no oil with them: But the wise took oil in their vessels with their lamps. While the bridegroom tarried, they all slumbered and slept. And at midnight, there was a cry made, Behold, the bridegroom cometh; go ye out to meet him. Then all those virgins arose, and trimmed their lamps. And the foolish said unto the wise, Give us of your oil; for our lamps are gone out. But the wise answered, saying, Not so; lest there be not enough for us and you: but go ye rather to them that sell, and buy for yourselves. And while they went to buy, the bridegroom came; and they that were ready went in with him to the marriage: and the door was shut. Afterward, came also the other virgins, saying, Lord, Lord, open to us. But he answered and said, Verily I say unto you, I know you not. Watch, therefore, for ye know neither the day nor the hour wherein the Son of man cometh (Matthew 25:1-13).

For the unsaved, consider your eternal destiny. Ensure your name is written in the Book of Life by accepting Jesus as your personal Lord and Savior. Luke 10:20 reminds us to rejoice because our names are written in heaven when we accept Christ. In Philippians 4:3, Paul acknowledges fellow believers whose names are in the Book of Life. It's time to secure your place in eternity by embracing the salvation offered through Jesus Christ.

Chapter 2

What is Heaven and Hell?

You might wonder, what exactly are heaven and hell, and why do they hold such significance? Heaven, a divine paradise, is where God resides. It is a beautiful, magnificent place where everything operates according to God's will. It is a place of love, peace, worship, serenity, community, tranquility and much more. It is a place where God is surrounded by His holy angels, heavenly beings, a heavenly court, gates of pearls, streets of gold etc.

And he carried me away in the spirit to a great high mountain, and shewed me that great city, the holy Jerusalem, descending out of heaven from God, Having the glory of God: and her light was like unto a stone most precious, even like a jasper stone, clear as crystal; And had a wall great and high, and had twelve gates, and at the gates twelve angels, and names written thereon, which are the names of the twelve tribes of the children of Israel: And the twelve gates were twelve pearls; every several gate was of one pearl: and the street of the city was pure gold, as it were transparent glass. And I saw no temple therein: for the Lord God Almighty and the Lamb are the temple of it.

And the city had no need of the sun, neither of the moon, to shine in it: for the glory of God did lighten it, and the Lamb is the light thereof (Rev. 21:10-12; 21-23).

Hell is a place of eternal darkness, fire, torment, misery, and punishment. Originally, it was not meant for man; it was prepared for satan and his fallen angels. However, those who choose to follow satan and reject God will also be cast into hell.

In hell, the lost soul will experience everlasting fire, with no end to suffering, pain, or torment. Every unrepentant, unsaved, ungodly soul will face judgment upon death, and their souls will be cast into the flames of eternal punishment.

And as it is appointed unto men once to die, but after this the judgement (Hebrews 9:27).

Then shall he say also unto them on the left hand, Depart from me, ye cursed, into everlasting fire, prepared for the devil and his angels. And these shall go away into everlasting punishment: but the righteous into life eternal (Matt 25:41, 46).

And shall cast them into a furnace of fire: there shall be wailing and gnashing of teeth (Matt. 13:42).

You must realize that hell will be a place where your worst nightmare and worst horror movie imaginable will come true. There will be no restraints and no limits to the amount of torment the demons of hell can inflict upon your soul. Once in, there is no getting out. Your soul will be eternally damned and lost for all eternity.

Remember, Jesus Christ said there would be wailing and gnashing of teeth.

Is There More to Know About Hell?

Indeed, the Bible reveals that hell has an ultimate destination. In the last days, many strange things will occur. At the very end of time, as we know it, the Bible describes what will happen to satan, his followers, and those who chose to serve him and receive the mark of the beast. Everything in hell will be cast into the lake of fire and brimstone, burning for eternity. This will be a far worse torment than hell itself. Can anyone imagine anything worse? The Word of God informs us that the devil, the beast, the false prophet, death, and hell will all be cast into the lake of fire and brimstone.

And the devil that deceived them was cast into the lake of fire and brimstone, where the beast and the false prophet are, and shall be tormented day and night for ever and ever. And death and hell were cast into the lake of fire. This is the second death. And whosoever was not found Written in the book of life was cast into the lake of fire" (Rev. 20:10, 14-15).

What Must I Do to Avoid Spending Eternity In Hell?

If you are thinking to yourself, I love the Lord and I don't want to spend eternity in hell. Then there is help for you. However, you must also be prepared to give up the world to follow Jesus. You need to be willing to die to self and its selfish desires and be open to accepting Jesus

Christ in your heart as your personal Lord and Savior.

In the scriptures, Jesus converses with a rich young ruler who asks Him what he must do to inherit eternal life. Initially, Jesus instructs him to keep the commandments, and then He challenges him to sell all his possessions and follow Him.

And, behold, one came and said unto him, Good Master, what good thing shall I do, that I may have eternal life? And he said unto him, Why callest thou me good? there is none good but one, that is, God: but if thou wilt enter into life, keep the commandments. He saith unto him, Which? Jesus said, Thou shalt do no murder, Thou shalt not commit adultery, Thou shalt not steal, Thou shalt not bear false witness, Honour thy father and thy mother: and, Thou shalt love thy neighbour as thyself. The young man saith unto him, All these things have I kept from my youth up: what lack I yet? Jesus said unto him, If thou wilt be perfect, go and sell that thou hast, and give to the poor, and thou shalt have treasure in heaven: and come and follow me. But when the young man heard that saying, he went away sorrowful: for he had great possessions (Matthew 19:16-22).

Jesus tested the young man to see where his heart really was. He wanted to know if the young man could give up all his earthly riches and become a disciple. Like many today, the young man could not let go of the things of this world in exchange for eternal life. The young man thought he was living a pretty good life, yet, as good as he was, his goodness could not get him into heaven. Life on earth is like a vapor; we are here today and gone tomorrow. The young man missed the point that when you die, you cannot take any earthly riches with you. The rich young ruler loved his wealth and the earthly things his wealth could buy him, yet he lost everything when he refused to let go of the things of this world and follow Jesus. In the end, the young man forfeited his eternal soul.

Chapter 3
Repentance

What is True Repentance?

Now that you understand the true meaning of salvation and have recognized your status as a sinner in need of salvation, the next crucial step is repentance. Repentance involves feeling genuine remorse for a life of sin, to the extent that you are willing to abandon wrongdoing and turn to Christ. It's essential to realize that the devil is not your friend; he aims to steal, kill, and destroy. However, Jesus Christ loves you and cares about the eternal destiny of your soul.

The thief cometh not, but for to steal, and to kill, and to destroy: I am come that they might have life, and that they might have it more abundantly (John 10:10).

According to John 10:10, the thief mentioned is the devil, while Jesus makes it clear that He came to offer abundant life. Repentance is not merely about acknowledging sin; it involves stepping out of the darkness into the marvelous light of God. Acts 3:19 emphasizes that repentance leads to the wiping out of sins and brings times of refreshing from the Lord. Transitioning from a life of sin to a life of righteousness through Jesus Christ is pivotal. God holds us accountable when we consciously commit sin. Once you recognize something as sin, avoid deliberate practice while assuming that repentance alone suffices. Authentic repentance involves a genuine commitment to renounce sin and seek forgiveness through the grace of Jesus Christ.

Repent ye therefore, and be converted, that your sins may be blotted out, when the times of refreshing shall come from the presence of the Lord (Acts 3:19).

Genuine repentance involves recognizing the depth of your sin and making a heartfelt commitment to forsake that lifestyle permanently. A biblical example highlights the contrasting outcomes of Judas and Peter. Judas, who betrayed Jesus, expressed regret but fell short of full repentance. His remorse led to a tragic end, as he hanged himself, showcasing the consequences of incomplete repentance.

Then Judas, which had betrayed Him, when he saw that he was condemned, repented himself, and brought again the thirty pieces of silver to the chief priests and elders, Saying, I have sinned in that I have betrayed innocent blood. And they said, what is that to us? See thou to that. And he cast down the pieces of silver in the temple, departed, and went and hanged himself (Matthew 27: 3-5).

In contrast, Peter, despite his love for the Lord, denied knowing Jesus three times out of fear. Yet, when confronted with his failure, he wept bitterly, showing deep sorrow and genuine repentance. God, seeing the sincerity of Peter's repentant heart, forgave him. The distinction between Judas and Peter lies in their intentions. Judas premeditated his betrayal for personal gain, while Peter, motivated by fear, did not plan to deny Jesus in advance.

Then began he to curse and to swear, saying, I know not the man. And immediately the cock crew. And peter remembered the word of Jesus, which said unto him, Before the cock crow, thou shalt deny me thrice. And he went out, and wept bitterly (Matthew 26: 74-75).

Continuing on the path of genuine repentance is an ongoing process that shapes the Christian journey. It entails a persistent commitment to righteousness, a continual turning away from sinful inclinations, and a sincere reliance on the grace of Jesus Christ.

True repentance involves not only recognizing specific sins but also addressing the root causes that may lead to repetitive transgressions. It requires a thorough self-examination, seeking God's guidance to identify patterns of behavior or thought that may hinder a complete transformation.

The biblical narrative of repentance emphasizes a turning not just from individual sins but from a life dominated by sin. In the case of Zacchaeus, a tax collector who encountered Jesus, his repentance extended beyond a mere acknowledgment of wrongdoing. He pledged to make amends for his dishonest gains and demonstrated a commitment to a new way of living.

And Zacchaeus stood, and said unto the Lord; Behold, Lord, the half of my goods I give to the poor; and if I have taken anything from any man by false accusation, I restore him fourfold. And Jesus said unto him, This day is salvation come to this house, forsomuch as he also is a son of Abraham (Luke 19:8-9).

This story illustrates the transformative power of repentance, showcasing that genuine remorse leads to tangible actions and a changed lifestyle. It is a continuous turning toward God and away from the allure of sin.

As you navigate the path of repentance, it is essential to lean on the support of the Holy

Spirit. The Holy Spirit plays a pivotal role in the process of sanctification, empowering believers to overcome the struggles associated with sin and aiding in the renewal of the mind.

And be not conformed to this world: but be ye transformed by the renewing of your mind, that ye may prove what is that good, and acceptable, and perfect, will of God (Romans 12:2).

Repentance involves aligning your mind, desires, and actions with God's will. It requires a surrender of your will to the guidance of the Holy Spirit, allowing Him to lead you into a life of righteousness. The process of sanctification is a cooperative effort between the believer and the Holy Spirit, marked by a continual turning away from sin and a pursuit of holiness.

In summary, true repentance is a dynamic and transformative journey, marked by a sincere commitment to forsake sin, ongoing self-examination, and reliance on the empowering grace of Jesus Christ. It involves not only acknowledging specific sins but also addressing underlying issues and patterns of behavior. As you embark on this journey, may the Holy Spirit guide you, empowering you to live a life that aligns with God's perfect will.

Chapter 4
Forgiveness

Why is Forgiveness So Important?

Forgiveness is a choice, and it is a crucial aspect of our Christian journey. While it's vital to forgive those who have caused us significant hurt, harm, or pain, depending on the offense, it can be challenging for the person who was harmed or offended. Sometimes, letting go of these feelings seems impossible.

To forgive means to stop feeling angry or resentful towards someone for an offense or mistake done to us by an individual or individuals. When you are unable to forgive, it puts you in bondage to that person or situation. Every time you see that person, you replay the event in your head. This means that encountering that person triggers uncontrollable emotions or unpleasant memories.

Yet, Jesus Christ requires us to forgive our enemies and those who trespass against us. The question is, why would Jesus place such a demand on us? The answer is simple. Even though His enemies hung Him on the cross, at the very end, He forgave them. Jesus didn't take time to look at his circumstances and have a pity party. Instead He chose to look beyond his on lookers and focus on the task ahead.

Then said Jesus, Father, forgive them; for they know not what they do. And they parted his raiment, and cast lots (Luke 23:34).

Are we any better than our Lord and Savior Jesus Christ? He gave his life as a ransom for humanity, taking our place and paying our sin debt in full by shedding his innocent blood on the cross. Only through the shedding of his blood on Calvary could unholy man be reconciled to Holy God.

Jesus endured a brutal night of pain, suffering, and torture, yet he had one mission in mind: to complete the work of the cross and bridge the gap between unholy man and Holy God. Jesus reminds us of what will happen if we refuse to forgive.

But if ye forgive not men their trespasses, neither will your Father forgive your trespasses (Matthew 6:15).

If you hold on to the bitterness, anger, rage, and evil ways, those things are not going to get into heaven. God is looking for someone with a broken and contrite spirit, someone who is willing to let go of the world to follow Jesus.

Remember, forgiveness is a choice. You must choose to forgive; you must choose to let it go. Once you surrender those emotions, hurt, and pain to Jesus, then He can begin the process of inner healing for you. He will set you free from all pain and suffering, whether emotional or physical. He can and will make you whole. But first, you must trust Him by standing on His word and believing Him to take you through the process of healing.

The story of Joseph and his brothers is a prime example of how forgiveness can shape our destiny. Joseph was attacked, thrown into a pit and sold into slavery by his older brothers. His brother's actions caused him years of slavery and imprisonment. He endured years of grief, suffering and pain, yet God wanted Joseph to forgive them for a greater purpose. Little did Joseph know that the entire future of Israel depended on his one act of forgiveness.

And it came to pass, when Joseph was come unto his brethren, that they stript Joseph out of his coat, his coat of many colours that was on him; And they took him, and cast him into a pit: and the pit was empty, there was no water in it. Then there passed by Midianites merchantmen; and they drew and lifted up Joseph out of the pit, and sold Joseph to the Ishmeelites for twenty pieces of silver: and they brought Joseph into Egypt (Genesis 37:23-24; 28).

Joseph's brothers sold him into slavery out of jealousy, unaware of the eventual outcome. God has a way of turning bad situations into opportunities for His glory, and in Joseph's case, there was a master plan.

God delivered Joseph from prison by enabling him to interpret a dream for Pharaoh that no one else could. As a result, Pharaoh elevated Joseph to the position of second in command.

And Pharaoh said unto Joseph, forasmuch as God hath shewed thee all this, there is none so discreet and wise as thou art: Thou shall be over my house, and according unto thy word shall all my people be ruled: only in the throne will I be greater than thou. And Pharaoh said unto Joseph, See, I have set thee over all the land of Egypt (Genesis 41: 39-41).

During a severe famine, Joseph's family journeyed to Egypt to buy corn, unaware that the high-ranking Egyptian official they encountered was their estranged brother. Joseph orchestrated events revealing his true identity. Afterwards, he sent for his father and relocated the entire family to Egypt. After their father's passing, Joseph's brothers approached him, seeking forgiveness for the grave injustice they had committed against him. In a moment of divine grace, Joseph chose compassion over vengeance, illustrating the transformative power of forgiveness even in the face of profound betrayal.

And when Joseph's brethren saw that their father was dead, they said, Joseph will peradventure hate us, and will certainly requite us all the evil we did unto him. And they sent a messenger unto Joseph, saying, Thy father did command before he died, saying, So shall ye say unto Joseph, Forgive, I pray thee now, the trespass of thy brethren, and their sin; for they did unto thee evil: and now, we pray thee, forgive the trespass of the servants of the God of thy father. And Joseph wept when they spake unto him. And his brethren also went and fell down before his

*face; and they said, Behold, we be thy servants.
And Joseph said unto them, Fear not: for am I in
the place of God? But as for you, ye thought evil
against me; but God meant it unto good, to bring
to pass, as it is this day, to save much people alive
(Genesis 50:15-20).*

In the narrative of Joseph, we witness a profound example of Jesus working from the inside out to heal emotional wounds. Just as Joseph found solace and liberation through forgiveness, you too can experience the transformative touch of Jesus. Unburden yourself from the weight of pain, hurt, and unforgiveness. Today, invite Jesus to mend the broken pieces within, allowing His divine grace to bring healing and restoration. Embrace the liberating power of forgiveness, and as you relinquish control, let God navigate through the complexities of life's challenges. Release the unsolvable problems into His capable hands, trusting that His love will guide you to a place of peace and wholeness.

Come unto me, all ye that labour and are heavy laden, and I will give you rest. Take my yoke upon you, and learn of me, for I am meek and lowly in heart: and ye shall fine rest unto your souls. For my yoke is easy, and my burden is light (Matthew 11:28-30).

The Effects of Unforgiveness

Holding on to unforgiveness is like cancer; it will eat away at the very core of your being. It tends to manifest physically in your body as sickness and emotionally in your mind as mental illness. The bitterness from unforgiveness will eat away at your soul. While releasing it may seem like giving the other person a pass, you're actually freeing yourself from bondage by satan. Unforgiveness gives satan an open door to come and go in your life at will, making you miserable.

Many good people in this world think they're going to heaven but still harbor bitterness and unforgiveness. Unfortunately, they are sadly mistaken. You don't want to have lived for Christ your entire life or have just given your life to Christ, only to stand before God and hear, "...*Depart from me, ye that work iniquity*" (Matthew 7:23). You might say, "Father, what iniquity?" He will say, "Your refusal to forgive." Don't let unforgiveness be the reason why your soul spends eternity in hell.

For we must all appear before the judgment seat of Christ; that every one may receive the things done in his body, according to that he hath done, whether it be good or bad (2 Cor. 5:10).

How Many Times Should We Forgive Lord?

Peter had a question to ask Jesus. He wanted to know if there was a limit on how many times he should forgive his brethren. Jesus gave Peter an unexpected answer.

Then came Peter to him, and said, Lord, how oft shall my brother sin against me, and I forgive him? till seven times? Jesus saith unto him, I say not unto thee, Until seven times: but, Until seventy times seven (Matthew 18:21-22).

It can be something that happened decades ago, or it can be a person who keeps repeating the same actions. You might have believed you got over it or let go of it until that situation resurfaces. Now, satan has you on an emotional roller coaster, and all the emotions come flooding back as if it happened yesterday. However, once you surrender that area to Christ, He will make it as if that situation never happened. You may ask yourself, "What if it's a close relative?" Here's the answer: take it to the cross, tell Jesus all about it, and once you're done, leave it there.

Dearly beloved, avenge not yourselves, but rather give place unto wrath: for it is written, Vengeance is mine; I will repay, saith the Lord (Romans 12:19).

Time To Separate

Forgiveness doesn't mean that you must keep putting yourself in a compromising position. There are times in our lives when we must forgive and separate simultaneously. In certain situations, it is necessary to distance ourselves from conflict to preserve our lives and maintain our joy. The Bible assures us that it is okay to cut ties with a person to safeguard our own souls. God will always provide a way out of a bad situation.

And if thy right hand offend thee, cut it off, and cast it from thee: for it is profitable for thee that one of thy members should perish, and not that thy whole body should be cast into hell (Matthew 5:30).

Forgiveness as an Act of Faith

Forgiveness, as an act of faith, involves navigating the complex terrain of hurt, betrayal, and emotional wounds. It acknowledges that we live in a fallen world where relationships can be sources of deep pain. Yet, even in the face of profound hurt, forgiveness calls us to trust in God's sovereignty and redemptive power.

Romans 8:28 assures believers that "*all things work together for good to them that love God, to them who are the called according to his purpose.*" This includes the pain caused by others. Forgiveness requires a belief that God can take even the most broken situations and weave them into a tapestry of redemption and growth.

Restoring Brokenness Through Faith

Forgiveness, grounded in faith, possesses a healing power that transcends human understanding. It allows God to restore what is broken and shattered. The process of forgiveness becomes a journey of faith where wounds are transformed into scars—reminders of God's redemptive work rather than sources of ongoing pain.

Colossians 3:13 provides a powerful exhortation: *"Forbearing one another, and forgiving one another, if any man have a quarrel against any: even as Christ forgave you, so also do ye."* This verse links the forgiveness we extend to others with the forgiveness we have received from the Lord. It's a reminder that our capacity to forgive is fueled by the understanding of the immense forgiveness we ourselves have experienced through Christ.

Praying for Those Who Hurt Us

An active demonstration of forgiveness as an act of faith is found in Jesus' command to pray for those who hurt us. In Matthew 5:44, Jesus instructs, "*But I say unto you, Love your enemies, bless them that curse you, do good to them that hate you, and pray for them which despitefully use you, and persecute you.*" Praying for those who have wronged us requires a deep reliance on God's grace and an acknowledgment that our ability to love our enemies is only possible through faith in Christ.

Faith-Fueled Forgiveness: A Continuous Journey, A Lifelong Commitment

Forgiveness as an act of faith is not a one-time event but a lifelong commitment. It involves repeatedly choosing faith over bitterness, trust over resentment. The journey of faith-fueled forgiveness may have setbacks, but the overarching theme is a persistent reliance on God's grace and a belief in His ability to bring beauty from ashes.

Casting Sins into the Depths of the Sea

Micah 7:18-19 beautifully encapsulates the essence of faith-fueled forgiveness: *"Who is a God like unto thee, that pardoneth iniquity, and passeth by the transgression of the remnant of his heritage? he retaineth not his anger for ever, because he delighteth in mercy. He will turn again, he will have compassion upon us; he will subdue our iniquities; and thou wilt cast all their sins into the depth of the sea."* This imagery reflects the profound nature of forgiveness rooted in faith—the casting away of sins, never to be retrieved or held against the forgiven.

Forgiveness as an act of faith is a dynamic, transformative journey. It involves trusting in God's sovereignty, surrendering the desire for personal vengeance, and actively participating in the redemptive work initiated by Christ's sacrificial forgiveness. It's a continuous process of entrusting brokenness to the Master Weaver, who, in His perfect wisdom, crafts a tapestry of redemption from the threads of forgiveness.

Chapter 5

Sinner's Prayer

The Best Choice: Receiving Salvation

The most profound decision one can make is to embrace salvation. As Jesus proclaimed, *"Now is the judgment of this world: now shall the prince of this world be cast out. And I, if I be lifted up from the earth, will draw all men unto me"* (John 12:31-32).

Upon receiving salvation, we not only renounce the influence of satan but also embrace the transformative power of Jesus Christ. It's a conscious decision to turn away from the darkness of sin and welcome the light of God's love into our lives. This act of surrender marks the beginning of a journey where we allow Jesus to guide our thoughts, actions, and decisions.

As we lift up Jesus in our hearts, His teachings, and His love become the driving force behind our existence. The promise of salvation not only secures our place in eternity but also grants us access to the abundant life that Jesus promised. By continually seeking Him and following His example, we become vessels of His grace, reflecting His light to the world around us.

Exalting Jesus is not a one-time event but a daily commitment. It involves living out our faith, sharing His love, and letting His transformative power shape every aspect of our lives. In doing so, we fulfill Jesus' promise—drawing others to Him through the undeniable presence of His love in our hearts

The Prayer of Salvation

Now, are you ready to receive salvation? Believing in Jesus Christ is the key. He is the Savior of the world, the one who died on the cross for your salvation. Put your faith in Him as your personal Lord and Savior. As you open your heart to receive Jesus, He will come in, cleanse you, and grant you the gift of eternal life.

Are you ready to give your heart to Christ?
If so, pray this prayer:

Dear heavenly Father, In Jesus name,

Lord, I come before you as humbly as I know

how. I realize I am a sinner in need of

salvation. Lord, come into my heart and save

my soul. I confess my sins to you and I repent

of all the sins I've ever committed. Lord I ask

you to forgive me of my sins and wash me in

your precious blood. Lord, I do believe that

you are the son of God and that you died on

the cross and rose on the third day. Cleanse

me Lord and make me whole. By faith I

renounce satan and his dark kingdom and

accept you Lord Jesus in my heart as my

personal Lord and Savior. Help me Lord to live

a holy life for you. Thank you for saving me.

In Jesus name I pray, Amen.

What's Next After Acceptance?

Now that you've accepted Jesus Christ personally, you've made the best decision of your life. You've been born again—a spiritual rebirth, as Jesus explained:

" ... *Except a man be born again, he cannot see the kingdom of God*" *(John 3:3).*

But as many as received him, to them gave he power to become the sons of God, even to them that believe on his name (John 1:12).

Because you are a newly converted child of God, it is a time of great joy and rejoicing. Jesus said:

Guard Your Soul

Having accepted Jesus Christ into your heart, it's essential to safeguard your soul. The most important and valuable possession you have is your soul. Once a person loses their soul, it is lost forever, and that person can never reclaim it. Once someone departs from this earth, they cannot return to negotiate with the devil for the return of their soul. No amount of money can repurchase it. Unfortunately, many famous and well-known people in today's society have traded their souls for fame and fortune.

Your soul is the essence of who you are –
your consciousness, identity, emotions, and will.
It continues to exist after the physical death of
your body.

God gave us free will, empowering us to
choose where our soul will spend eternity. Your
soul is more important than life itself. Life is like a
vapor, here today and gone tomorrow. Your
earthly life will end when you die, but your soul
lives on beyond death and is eternal.

Reflecting on the transient nature of life,
James 4:14 reminds us, "*Whereas ye know not
what shall be on the morrow. For what is your
life? It is even a vapour, that appeareth for a little
time, and then vanisheth away.*"

The devil, aware of his limited time and final destination in the lake of fire and brimstone, seeks to deceive as many unsuspecting souls as possible. Individuals who accept satan's offer of fame and fortune often forget that they cannot carry any earthly possessions beyond death.

Acknowledging the truth of 1 Timothy 6:7, *"For we brought nothing into this world, and it is certain we can carry nothing out,"* emphasizes the temporary nature of material possessions.

Revelation 20:10 depicts the ultimate fate of the devil who deceived humanity: *"And the devil that deceived them was cast into the lake of fire and brimstone, where the beast and the false prophet are, and shall be tormented day and night for ever and ever."*

We must be aware of the soul's value, refraining from selling it to the devil or handling it carelessly. Vigilantly guarding our souls involves loving God, as stated in Joshua 23:11.

When someone sells their soul, they trade it for temporary gratification. While it may appear that they gain the whole world, in the end, they lose both life and soul to satan. There is nothing that can be traded in exchange for the soul. Once forfeited to Satan, there is no turning back, and there is no "get out of hell" card.

Reflect on this deep truth: "*For what shall it profit a man, if he shall gain the whole world, and lose his own soul? Or what shall a man give in exchange for his soul*" (Mark 8:36-37)?

Chapter 6

Living the Christian Life

Sanctification

At times, we wonder about the meaning of sanctification. Essentially, it means the state or process of being free from sin, purified, and set apart for holy use by God. It signifies that you are a special vessel of God, and He has a divine purpose for your life. To live a sanctified life, you must make up your mind to separate from sin and disconnect from a sinful lifestyle. Because God gave us free will, this process will require deliberate action on our part.

Sanctify them through thy truth: thy word is truth (John 17:17).

For by one offering he hath perfected for ever them that are sanctified (Hebrews 10:14).

And such were some of you: but ye are washed, but ye are sanctified, but ye are justified in the name of the Lord Jesus, and by the Spirit of our God (1 Cor. 6:11).

Once you come to know Jesus, this process becomes easier because He gives you a new heart, a renewed mind, a new way of thinking, and new desires. We are called to have the mind and attitude of Jesus Christ.

Therefore if any man be in Christ, he is a new creature: old things are passed away; behold, all things are become new (2 Corinthians 5:17).

Let this mind be in you that was also in Christ Jesus (Phil. 2:5).

To have the mind of Jesus, it's crucial to examine His heart towards His fellow man. He embodied humility, selflessness, a willingness to serve others, and demonstrated obedience all the way to the cross, where He selflessly laid down His life for mankind.

Taking the Next Step: Baptism After Salvation

Now that you've received salvation, the question arises: What's the next step? It is recommended to undergo baptism, as it serves as a public confession of your faith in Jesus Christ. By being baptized, you are proclaiming your commitment to follow Jesus. Baptism symbolizes Christ's death on the cross, burial, and resurrection from the dead. As you are immersed in water, it signifies the burial of your old life. Rising from the water symbolizes the resurrection, depicting God's transformation from death to a new life in Christ. Through baptism, you declare to the world that you now lead a new life as a Christian.

The Scriptures affirm this symbolism:

Therefore, we are buried with him by baptism into death: that like as Christ was raised up from the dead by the glory of the Father, even so we also should walk in the newness of life (Romans 6:4).

Additionally Jesus, in His final commission, urged His followers:

Go, therefore, and make disciples of all the nations, baptizing them in the name of the Father and the Son and the Holy Spirit (Matthew 28:19).

Baptism becomes a significant step in your Christian journey—a step of obedience, public testimony, and alignment with the transformative work of Christ in your life.

Navigating Your Journey as a Christian

As a new Christian, the next step is important. Immerse yourself in the Word of God through daily Bible reading and study. Understanding the Scriptures is essential in deepening your relationship with God. As you engage in regular reading, the Holy Spirit will illuminate passages, enriching your understanding of His Word. Remember, as a follower of Christ, you'll inevitably encounter questions about your faith. Can you confidently share the truth about who Jesus is?

Thy word have I hid in mine heart, that I might not sin against thee. Blessed art thou, O Lord; teach me thy statutes (Psalms 119:11-12).

Study to shew thyself approved unto God, a workman that needeth not to be ashamed, rightly dividing the word of truth (2 Timothy 2:15).

Now, as a Christian, develop a habit of daily prayer. Prayer is transformative—it shifts mindsets, softens hearts, and alters circumstances. It's your intimate connection with the Lord, a time to nurture a personal relationship with Jesus Christ.

Reflecting and meditating on Scripture is equally important. To meditate means to think deeply or focus one's mind on something. In this case, you are carefully focusing your mind on the holy scriptures. As you begin your journey of meditating on the Word of God and communing with Him daily in prayer, you will find yourself growing in grace and becoming stronger in God's word and in your Christian experience.

Do not be anxious about anything, but in every situation, by prayer and petition, with thanksgiving, present your requests to God (Philippians 4:6).

And he spake a parable unto them to this end, that men ought always to pray, and not to faint (Luke 18:1).

This book of the law shall not depart out of thy mouth; but thou shalt meditate therein day and night, that thou mayest observe to do according to all that is written therein; for then thou shalt make thy way prosperous, and then thou shalt have good success (Joshua 1:8).

Embrace this journey of spiritual growth with eagerness and commitment, knowing that

God's Word and prayer will guide and strengthen you every step of the way.

Christian Misconceptions

There are many Christian misconceptions. Some people think that attending church makes them a Christian. However, attending church does not make you a Christian. Just because you joined a church and repeated the sinner's prayer behind someone who instructed you to do so does not make you a Christian. Even if your mom or dad is a Christian or a church leader, it does not make you one. You must accept Jesus Christ into YOUR heart through faith and seek forgiveness for YOUR sins. You must have a personal relationship with the Lord for YOURSELF. It is YOUR soul we are talking about here, not someone else's. The Bible tells us to study to show ourselves approved. How can you say you are a Christian if you don't even know what is in the most important book in Christianity—the Bible? The Bible lets us know that the Bereans searched the Scriptures daily to see if what the Apostle Paul was preaching was true.

And the brethren immediately sent away Paul and Silas by night into Berea: who coming thither went into the synagogue of the Jews. These were more noble than those in Thessalonica, in that they received the word with all readiness of mind, and searched the scriptures daily, whether those things were so (Acts 17:10-11).

Once you study the Word of God for yourself, it will be hard for someone to deceive you. Many are deceived because they rely on the knowledge of others. The Lord wants His people to know and understand His Word for themselves. As we develop our prayer life, we can ask God to reveal His Word to us by giving us wisdom, knowledge, and divine revelation.

The fear of the Lord is the beginning of knowledge. But fools despise wisdom and instruction (Proverbs 1:7).

Wisdom is the principal thing; therefore get wisdom: and with all thy getting get understanding (Proverbs 4:7).

If any of you lack wisdom, let him ask God, that giveth to all men liberally, and upbraideth not; and it shall be given him (James 1:5).

The following statement, "Once saved always saved," is yet another of the many Christian misconceptions believed by a lot of people today.

Once Saved Always Saved?

Many people feel that once you are saved you are always saved no matter what you do. They feel that being saved gives them card blanche to attend church and still live a life of sin and disobedience to God. Although they proclaim to be a Christian, they continue to live their lives in a backslidden state as if they never knew God at all. Many are Christian in name only. They are not Christ like in the way they live their everyday lives.

The Bible lets us know that if you do not remain faithful to God and go back into the world to serve the devil, you run the risk of losing your very soul. If a person has once known God and die in a backslidden state without having time to repent, they will be judged. *Hebrews 9:27 says, "And as it is appointed unto men once to die, but after this the judgement."*

An additional scenario arises during the reign of the Antichrist. Individuals may face a choice: renounce Christ or face death. In such circumstances, those who had accepted Christ earlier in their life could lose their salvation by turning away from Christ and choosing to serve satan and accept the mark of the beast. In such cases it is not, "Once saved, always saved."

Revelations 14:9-11 vividly describes the consequences for those who choose to worship the beast and accept its mark. This scripture underscores the importance of unwavering faith and adherence to God's commandments.

And the third angel followed them, saying with a loud voice, If any man worship the beast and his image, and receive the mark in his forehead, or in his hand, The same shall drink of the wine of the wrath of God, which is poured out without mixture into the cup of his indignation; and he shall be tormented with fire and brimstone in the presence of the holy angels, and in the presence of the Lamb: And the smoke of their torment ascendeth up for ever and ever: and they have no rest day nor night, who worship the beast and his image, and whosoever receiveth the mark of his name. Here is the patience of the saints: here are they that keep the commandments of God, and the faith of Jesus (Revelations 14:9-11).

Revelations 13:8 further reinforces the gravity of the choice, stating, *"And all that dwell upon the earth shall worship him, whose names are not written in the book of life of the Lamb slain from the foundation of the world."*

The bible reminds us that once you accept the mark of the beast, you are eternally lost. Remember, at that time in history, when the antichrist is revealed, you must not accept the mark of the beast. If any Christian have known God for 30 or 40 years, the moment you accept the mark, you are renouncing your Lord and Savior Jesus Christ and agreeing that satan is now your new Lord and indicating that you are willing to join satan in the lake of fire and brimstone. This highlights the significance of regularly attending church and immersing oneself in the Word of God. These practices contribute to building a steadfast faith that withstands challenges and temptations.

Why Should I Meet Regularly With Other Christians?

The Bible encourages believers not to forsake assembling together (Hebrews 10:25). Once you begin your Christian walk, you will want to meet other Christians. Attending Sunday School, regular church services, Bible study, and prayer meetings are all good ways to associate with other Christians. Sometimes, someone else may have already experienced something you are presently struggling with and can provide words of encouragement to help you better work through your problems. The purpose of assembling together is to receive strength and inspiration from others in the faith.

Not forsaking the assembling of ourselves together, as the manner of some is, but exhorting one another: and so much the more, as ye see the day approaching (Hebrews 10:25).

In conclusion, the Christian journey goes beyond a one-time decision; it requires ongoing commitment, steadfastness, and active participation in a faith community. Let us debunk misconceptions and strive for a faith that endures, rooted in a continuous relationship with Christ and fellow believers.

Chapter 7

The Holy Spirit

What is the Holy Spirit?

Contrary to popular misconceptions, the Holy Spirit is not an "It." He is a person with agency and purpose. He is the third person in the Trinity, consisting of God the Father, God the Son, and God the Holy Spirit. The Holy Spirit plays a significant role in the conversion of each sinner. He convicts the sinner of unrighteousness and sin, leading them to salvation by revealing who Jesus is and the work of the cross. Without Him, sinners could not be drawn to the cross. The Holy Spirit's work shows sinners the error of their ways through reproof and correction.

Through the redeeming work of the Holy Spirit, the believer is united with Jesus Christ and positioned in the church, which is the body of Christ. Upon conversion, the Holy Spirit indwells the born-again believer, enabling and equipping them to live a victorious life in Christ. He is the one who executes the power. Jesus was raised from the dead by the resurrection power of the Holy Spirit.

Not by works of righteousness which we have done, but according to his mercy he saved us, by the washing of regeneration, and renewing of the Holy Ghost (Titus 3:5).

Even the Spirit of truth, whom the world cannot receive, because it seeth him not, neither knoweth him; for he dwelleth with you, and shall be in you (John 14:17).

But if the same Spirit that raised up Jesus from the dead dwell in you, he that raised up Christ from the dead shall also quicken your mortal bodies by his Spirit that dwelleth in you (Romans 8:11).

As Christian believers, we are to lift up the name of Jesus every chance we get by proclaiming the good news of the gospel. We are to be witnesses for Jesus in this fallen world, letting sinners know that Jesus saves and is concerned about them. When we open our mouths and talk about the goodness of Jesus and the work of the cross, our lives become a testimony. At that point, the Holy Spirit will do His job and begin to attract men and women to Jesus Christ. Jesus Himself tells us what He will do if He is lifted up.

And I, if I be lifted up from the earth, will draw all men unto me (John 12:32).

Speaking in Tongues

Now that you have been converted, every Christian needs to go one step further and become baptized and filled with the Holy Spirit with the evidence of speaking in tongues. Just as the Bible is a weapon for every believer to have in their arsenal, it is the Word of God—a sword for every believer. The enemy, satan, has no recourse against it. The Bible is the living Word of God, making satan weak and stripping him of his power. The Holy Spirit is another weapon against satan.

When you begin to pray in tongues or your heavenly prayer language, your mind is unfruitful. This means you are uttering words and communicating with God in a language unknown to you and beyond your natural understanding. This can be done in private prayer time, as it is direct communication between you and God. Praying in tongues is essential to the Christian believer's walk in the Spirit. Through this avenue, the Lord will give us divine revelation, quicken our spirit, and build us up in our faith as He speaks and communes with our inner selves.

It is also a good idea to wait on the Lord for a response. Often, as you listen, the Lord will begin to speak to your heart—words of comfort, words of encouragement, or prophetic words. Those are times to have pen and paper ready to journal. Many times, we do not know what we are to pray about, but the Holy Spirit makes intercession for our spirit. During this intimate prayer time, the Holy Spirit prays the perfect prayer on our behalf. This prayer can be prayed as often as you deem necessary. It is the one prayer that satan cannot sabotage or interfere with because he does not know what the Holy Spirit is saying to God on your behalf.

For he that speaketh in an unknown tongue speaketh not unto men, but unto God: for no man understandeth him; howbeit in the spirit he speaketh mysteries (1Cor. 14:2).

For if I pray in an unknown tongue, my spirit prayeth, but my understanding is unfruitful (1Cor. 14:14).

I thank God that, I speak with tongues more than ye all (1Cor. 14:18).

But ye, beloved, building up yourselves on your most holy faith, praying in the Holy Ghost (Jude 20).

Equipping of the Saints

The Holy Spirit equips the saints for service in the work of the Lord. There are nine gifts of the Holy Spirit, and each gift helps the believer overcome the obstacles sent their way by satan.

The nine gifts of the Holy Spirit are: The word of wisdom, the word of knowledge, faith, gifts of healing, working of miracles, prophecy, discerning of spirits, divers kinds of tongues, interpretation of tongues. These spiritual gifts are given to the believer to edify and build up others. They are given to edify and build up the church. These gifts are distributed by the Holy Spirit of God to aid in ministering to the unsaved and the lost souls.

The word of wisdom is when the Holy Spirit imparts the wisdom of God about a situation. It is a way in which the truth of God is shared with men in a truthful and understandable way.

Through wisdom is an house builded; and by understanding it is established: and by knowledge shall the chambers be filled with all precious and pleasant riches. A wise man is strong; yea, a man of knowledge increaseth strength. For by wise counsel thou shalt make thy war: and in multitude of counsellors there is safety (Proverbs 24:3-6).

Counsel is mine, and sound wisdom: I am understanding; I have strength (Proverbs 3:19).

If any of you lack wisdom, let him ask of God, that giveth to all men liberally, and upbraideth not; and it shall be given him (James 1:5).

The word of knowledge is supernaturally revealed knowledge of a particular situation or circumstances known only to God. This knowledge is revealed by the Holy Spirit to man for a specific purpose. It is God letting man know what to do in certain situations. It is knowledge that a person would not ordinarily know unless it is revealed by the Holy Spirit of God.

Jesus answered them, and said, My doctrine is not mine, but his that sent me. If any man will do his will, he shall know of the doctrine, whether it be of God, or whether I speak of myself (John 7:16-17).

Happy is the man that findeth wisdom, and the man that getteth understanding (Proverbs 3:13).

The gift of faith is supernaturally given by the Holy Spirit to the believer to believe God for the impossible in a given situation. This is unshakable faith that moves mountains in one's life. This goes beyond regular faith. It is strong, solid, and unwavering faith. This faith allows the Christian believer to do great things for God. With this faith, you don't concentrate on your circumstances or the situation around you; you only focus on the word and the promises of God. This faith takes God out of a box and removes all limitations.

And Jesus answering saith unto them, Have faith in God (Mark 11:22).

If ye have faith as a grain of mustard seed, ye shall say unto this mountain, Remove hence to yonder place; and it shall remove; and nothing shall be impossible unto you (Matthew 17:20).

Jesus said unto him, If thou canst believe, all things are possible to him that believeth (Mark 9:23).

The gift of healing is the supernatural ability given by God to impart healing to the physical body at a specific time. The gift of healing operates along with the gifts of faith and knowledge. It manifests as faith and knowledge are demonstrated, causing the individual being prayed for to be lifted up out of the realm of disbelief into the realm of healing and wholeness.

To another faith by the same spirit; to another the gifts of healing by the same spirit (1 Cor. 12:9).

And when he had called unto him his twelve disciples, he gave them power against unclean spirits, to cast them out, and to heal all manner of sickness and all manner of disease (Matthew 10:1).

The gift of the working of miracles is the supernatural working of God's Holy Spirit. It is when He performs such a mind-boggling miracle that it defies the laws of nature and gravity. It could appear as miraculous deliverance from a terrible situation, such as a storm or accident.

God also bearing them witness, both with signs and wonders, and with divers miracles, and gifts of the Holy Ghost, according to His own will (Hebrews 2:4).

This beginning of miracles did Jesus in Cana of Galilee, and manifested forth His glory; and His disciples believed on Him (John 2:11).

The gift of prophecy is when one speaks under the supernatural influence of the Holy Spirit. It is when God's word is spoken directly as the Holy Spirit reveals it to the church. To prophesy is to hear from God and to speak forth what God is saying. Thus, you are speaking the mind of God as He reveals it to you. God will often give the believer a glimpse into the future to prepare an individual or the church for things that are to come.

But he that prophesieth speaketh unto men to edification, and exhortation, and comfort (1Cor. 14:3).

For the testimony of Jesus is the spirit of prophesy (Rev. 19:10).

The gift of discerning of spirits is the supernatural work of the Holy Spirit that enables the believer to determine between good and evil. Is this of God or not? It keeps the believer from being deceived and led astray by the enemy. This gift helps the believer identify and recognize different spirits that are behind various manifestations in a variety of situations.

Beloved, believe not every spirit, but try the spirits whether they are of God: because many false prophets are gone out into the world (1 John 4:1).

Having a form of Godliness, but denying the power thereof: from such turn away (2 Timothy 3:5).

The gift of divers kinds of tongues is the God-given supernatural ability to speak or communicate in a language the believer does not know. This communication is to be interpreted in the gathering so everyone present will understand. It is a supernatural manifestation of the Holy Spirit through the person's speech organs. When this gift is used in private, it is for self-edification, but when used in public or a church gathering, it is to be interpreted to bless the people present.

To another working of miracles; to another prophecy; to another discerning of spirits; to another divers kinds of tongues; to another the interpretation of tongues (1 Cor. 12:10).

The gift of interpretation of tongues is the supernatural impulsive ability given by the Holy Spirit to an individual to interpret what someone is communicating in a meeting or church setting. An individual or persons in the meeting will be able to interpret what was spoken in tongues into a language easily understood by the people present. It must be understood that this gift has nothing to do with what someone naturally knows about a language. It comes directly from the Holy Spirit and is inspired by the Holy Spirit. Once the message is given in tongues, the interpretation should be given right away in response to the message given in tongues.

Wherefore let him that speaketh in an unknown tongue pray that he may interpret (1 Cor. 14:13)

If any man speak in an unknown tongue, let it be by two, or at the most by three, and that by course; and let one interpret (1 Cor. 14:27).

Chapter 8

Become a Soul Winner

Embracing the Call to Share the Good News

Now that you have read this book, it's time to go out into the world and help someone else. There are many people out there who would come to Christ if they only knew how. They would gladly turn to Jesus if they had someone to guide them along the way. This book serves as a valuable tool to lead family members, friends, colleagues, and associates to the redemptive grace of Jesus Christ.

Christianity is never to be forced on anyone, aligning with God's gift of free will. In the Garden of Eden, even Adam and Eve exercised their free will, choosing to disobey God and face the consequences. Their disobedience initiated a chain of events, leading humanity into a fallen state dominated by sin and death.

The concept of dominion, originally bestowed upon Adam and Eve, marked them as rulers over Earth. However, through deception, satan seized this dominion, becoming the prince of the air.

Wherein in time past ye walked according to the course of this world, according to the prince of the power of the air, the spirit that now worketh in the children of disobedience (Ephesians 2:2).

Yet, amidst Satan's treachery, God had a master plan of redemption. His profound love led to the sacrificial death of Jesus Christ, reconciling humanity with a holy God. As Christian believers, we are commissioned to be soul winners, adhering to the Great Commission. Our task is to spread the gospel, reflecting the love and redemption offered through Jesus Christ.

Matthew 28:19-20 outlines this divine command, emphasizing the importance of teaching and baptizing all nations. As we lift up the name of Jesus, He, in turn, draws people to

Himself. John 12:32 emphasizes this divine drawing, underscoring our chosen status in John 15:16.

Go ye therefore, and teach all nations, baptizing then in the name of the Father, and of the Son, and of the Holy Ghost. Teaching then to observe all things whatsoever I have commanded you: and, lo, I am with you always, even unto the end of the world. Amen (Matthew 28:19-20).

And I, if I be lifted up from the earth, will draw all men unto me (John 12:32).

Ye have not chosen me, but I have chosen you, and ordained you, that ye should go and bring forth fruit, and that your fruit should remain: that whatsoever ye shall ask of the Father in my name, he may give it you (John 15:16).

In these critical times, we must recognize the urgency of our mission. John 9:4 reminds us of the importance of working while it is day, for the night is coming. As we embark on this journey, the Our Father Prayer, taught by Jesus, becomes a powerful companion, guiding us in constant communication with our heavenly Father.

Our Father which art in heaven, Hollowed be thy name. Thy kingdom come. Thy will be done in earth, as it is in heaven. Give us this day our daily bread. And forgive our debts, as we forgive our debtors. And lead us not into temptation, but deliver us from evil: For thine is the kingdom, and the power, and the glory, for ever. Amen (Matt. 6:9-13).

I hope this book helps you along life's journey. Remember, we are like pilgrims passing through. Only what we do for God will count in the end. Be blessed.

Sinner's prayer

Dear heavenly Father, In Jesus name,

Lord, I come before you as humble as I know how.

I realize I am a sinner in need of salvation. Lord,

come into my heart and save my soul. I confess my

sins to you and I repent of all the sins I've ever

committed. Lord I ask you to forgive me of my sins

and wash me in your precious blood. Lord I do

believe that you are the son of God and that you

died on the cross and rose on the third day. Cleanse

me Lord and make me whole. By faith I renounce

satan and his dark kingdom and accept you Lord

Jesus in my heart as my personal Lord and Savior.

Help me Lord to live a holy life for you. Thank you

for saving me.

In Jesus name I pray, Amen.

www.ingramcontent.com/pod-product-compliance
Lightning Source LLC
Chambersburg PA
CBHW052108150726
48002CB00006B/2273